SEEKING

IMMORTALITY

Edward John Dawkins

First published in Great Britain as a hardback original in 2021

Copyright © Edward John Dawkins

The moral right of this author has been asserted.

Typeset in Book Antiqua

Design, typesetting and publishing by UK Book Publishing

www.ukbookpublishing.com

ISBN: 978-1-914195-83-9

CONTENTS

CONTENTS

INTRODUCTION

Throughout my life I have written poems, primarily funny little pieces of verse or short poems, that I wrote in friends' and relatives' birthday cards and in colleagues' retirement cards, however, I always wanted to write a book of poems, but never found the time to do this until I retired from work.

The next problem that I had was what would the poems be about. As a person born in 1949 I had a lifetime of experiences to draw upon, but I didn't want the poems to be just stories of my life put into verse. I wanted my poems not only to be interesting but also to make those who would read them stop and think about their "Life" and their life experiences. I hope that those who read these poems will, therefore, find them thought provoking and bring back memories of their own life, which was my aim. I have interspersed the more serious poems with light-hearted ones, yet even these I hope will be a little bit thought provoking.

So, dear reader, I hope you find my poems "interesting" and that they make you stop and think.

(N.B. All the poems were either written or started before the start of the Covid-19 pandemic that hit the United Kingdom at the beginning of 2020).

Edward John Dawkins

July 2021

SEEKING IMMORTALITY

When life is done
and our breath no longer moves the air,
When our dreams for our future are no more
and we lie at rest and cold;
Will the world remember our mundane lives
and our being here be forgotten ?
Will all that we were be gone forever
and our story never told ?

Can we make no mark upon this earth,
Must our existence be erased ?
What legacy will we leave behind
As our souls into eternity fade ?

Till the end of time we can only leave our words behind
To live on beyond the grave;
To tell the generations still to come
Of who we were and how we spent our days.

So I say to you, fellow traveller, leave some words behind
To tell the future of your thoughts and of your reality,
And of the poignant lessons that you learned in life,
Maybe then you'll have a chance of immortality.

E J Dawkins

OH I WISH I WERE A BOY AGAIN

Oh I wish I were a boy again,
A time when I was not yet ten;
Wrapped in love in my mother's arms,
I wish I could go back there again.

Oh I wish I were a boy again,
When cares and worries were unknown,
When the sun seemed to shine most every day
And I had no misfortunes to bemoan.

Oh I wish I were a boy again,
Young and reckless, running wild, running free;
Playing games with the kids out in the street,
But always back home, by five o'clock,
for jam sandwiches and tea.

Oh I wish I were a boy again,
When the future was so far away,
When the flavours of life were truly savoured
And tomorrow was more than just another day.

You my think that my wish is foolish,
That I look back to that time only with
nostalgia, forgetting any hurt and pain;
This may be true, but like well loved nursery rhymes,
Only happy memories of my boyhood
remain, embedded deeply in my brain.

Every child deserves a carefree childhood,
Though sadly for too many this isn't so,
But my childhood was full of fun and fascination
So that's why, back there, it's where I want to go.

E J Dawkins

MEMORIES

Our memories are who we are,
Collected from our very start,
When in our mother's womb we laid
And listened to her beating heart.

Next we store memories of our childhood days
Which shaped our lives and, with learning, filled our brain;
Of feeling every emotion when playing playground games
And when our peers and parents taught
us the meaning of joy and pain.

Then memories of those intense adolescent days
When a rush of hormones our bodies changed,
When thoughts of sex consumed our brain,
And the mating game nearly drove us insane.

Our first day at work we all can recall,
No longer a child playing the fool;
Building a career every working day,
Then, at weekends, adult games we'd play.

Years spent settling down in married life,
Young lovers still, but now husband and wife.
Days spent striving for the best,
Building a home, a place to nest.

Then those happy days spent with children,
Nurturing them as they grew and grew,
From infancy to maturity,
Nervously watching as the nest they flew.

(Continued)

Life then continued in a different way,
With new events and knowledge to be filed away,
Constantly collecting memories day by day
Hoping that the best would not fade away;

And in old age we need our lifetime's memories the most
To remind us of who we are and what
we've done and where we've been
To pass on to those who'll listen, our
thoughts, our knowledge, our history
But we need them most of all for when
we close our eyes and dream.

E J Dawkins

EMOTIONS

Emotions are sensations that well up from within us;
They make us human, they help to make us who we are,
They come and go with the events of each new day,
But dealing with them is our toughest job by far !

E J Dawkins

BALL OF FLUFF

In my hand it laid asleep that day,
A tiny ball of fluff;
New to the world and to the day,
Just a tiny ball of fluff.

It stretched out a paw and opened an eye,
Then it went to sleep once more;
And with shallowed breath I watched it sleep,
Gently stroking its outstretched paw.

A whisker twitched, its body shook;
Was their anguish in its dream ?
Then, with eyes closed, it smiled,
Then licked its nose,
Was it dreaming of some cream ?

E J Dawkins

OUT IN THE OPEN AIR

Going for a walk, a ramble, a stroll
Does something for the mind, the body, the soul,
One foot following the other out in the open air,
The mind calms, the body relaxes, the
soul rejoices stripped of care.

To take a walk down a familiar or unknown street,
Not knowing what you'll see or who'll meet,
Will quickly break the chain of unwelcome
thoughts within your mind
As you begin to notice interesting
everyday things of many kinds.

To ramble across fields and vales and hills
Is simply for the senses a total thrill.
To see nature at its glorious best
Is a pleasure unsurpassed by all the rest.

To stroll along a river bank or ocean shore
Is a spiritual treat when in the great outdoors.
For the tranquility of a river and the serenity of the sea
Will enter your soul and set your spirit free.

No matter what the season, no matter what the hour
Be it in sunshine, moonshine, snow,
hail, wind or a gentle shower,
To take a walk beneath a daytime sky
or nighttime star lit heaven
Is a gift that, from infancy to frail old
age, we've all been given.

For there is no greater joy in life
Than to feel the ground pass beneath your feet
As you stride out in the open air
And to feel your spirits rise with every heartbeat.

E J Dawkins

THE EYES OF A LITTLE CHILD

When I look into the eyes of a little child
Let me tell you what I see,
Two trusting, innocent, orbs
Looking quizzically back at me.

With no wisdom, just questioning curiosity
They look out at each new day,
And bewildered they seek assurance
To make uncertainty go away.

When happy they sparkle
Like moonlight on the sea;
When sad they become misty
And oh so melancholy.

In an instant they can melt
A selfish ice-cold heart,
And with one pleading look
Tear angry rage apart.

They can only tell the truth,
They have not yet learned to lie,
And when shedding a gentle tear
They can make the whole world cry.

E J Dawkins

AMELIE

(My granddaughter)

She wakes up from a dream or two,
But the light's too bright for her to see,
Then rubbing her eyes with little fists
She smiles as she looks at me.

And in those eyes there is instant joy,
She has no worries of the grown-up everyday;
A tiny tot just two years old,
Who, like me in days of old, only wants to play.

"Gandad" she shouts as I reach out to her
For a kiss and a welcoming cuddle,
But there are more interesting things than me
for her to do and see,
So in seconds all her toys are out
and the whole room's in a muddle.

This blue eyed, round faced little imp
Can do no wrong by me,
And as she trots around the house
She fills each room with glee.

Oh Amelie, sweet Amelie, with eyes so bright,
I wonder how your life will be ?
Oh Amelie, dear Amelie, with sparkling smile,
You mean the world to me.

Love "Gandad"

E J Dawkins

WHAT IS LOVE ?

What is this mysterious thing that we call Love ?
This question down the ages has constantly been asked.
Many a philosopher has tried to provide an answer,
But to put Love into words is simply an impossible task.

Yet I, who, like many, have lived a life
Full of joys and full of woes,
Can tell you this of Love from that
Which my passing years have let me know.

Love is a giddying emotion,
An unending yearning, a life long bond,
Love is far more than what the dictionary coldly states,
That Love is just "a feeling of deep affection".

Love is the constant that continues
after youthful passions fade
And the excitement of each new romance, sadly, is no more.
Love is a lasting devotion that holds you strong and fast
To that special one that you spent
so many years looking for.

Love is to care for, protect and cherish
Those deepest in your heart;
Love is praying to hold them tight again
Whenever you've been forced apart.

Love is the reason to be alive,
To live for each new day.
Love is the reason to endure
The bad things that happen along life's way.

Love is the one thing that
Beyond the grave lives on;
Yet many don't truly know what Love is
Until those that they have loved are gone.

E J Dawkins

THE MOMENT I MET MY WIFE

I met her at a ballroom dance class,
We were there to learn to dance.
Fate, they say, bring lovers together,
Or is it just one of life's games of chance.

She sat alone behind a small table
Nervously trying not to look into anyone's eyes,
But I'm sure that I saw her glance my way
Which took me, pleasantly, by surprise.

I told the young braves with whom I came
That I liked the look of the girl with the dusky hair,
But they said that she looked too good for me
And to ask her for a dance I wouldn't dare.

So with bravado I walked up to her table
Looking past her, pretending not to see her there,
Then I smiled at her and said hello or something
And casually, I thought, sat down next
to her in an empty chair.

We talked, then as we were called to the dance floor
I reached, fumbling, for her hand
And something about the warmth and softness of her skin
Caused a strange sensation inside me
that I didn't quite understand.

(Continued)

We walked tentatively to the dance floor
Then I turned and held her close
And the scent of her hair and the
firmness of her young body
Gave my heart an adrenaline overdose.

My mind couldn't hear the music or
obey the teacher's commands
And we stumbled awkwardly, and out of time,
through all of our first dance;
For all that I could think about was this
gorgeous creature in my arms
And the tender kiss that I would give
her when I had the chance.

E J Dawkins

OUT INTO THE WORLD

(Written for my niece)

Out into the world she went,
Her parents gave her their consent;
A young woman now, but inside still a girl,
Dreaming that her future would be a merry whirl.

Her days of childhood were all gone,
To the past they would now belong;
But had she learned those playground lessons well?
The future, unknown, would not yet tell.

And had older and wiser heads
Told her of what would lie ahead?
Times of great joy and times of despair,
The tests and temptations that would wait for her there;
The bad days when she would feel as if she were in a war,
The good days that she would remember for evermore.

And as for emotions that she would feel every day,
Had they told her that the strongest,
called love, could sweep her away?
And would she heed the warning given to every girl
When the girl became a Mademoiselle -
"Be careful, dear child, be as careful as you can,
Before you give your heart to any man".

E J Dawkins

I WAS YOUNG ONCE

(Written for my son and grandson)

"I was young once," said the old man to the youth,
"I too dreamed of love, luxury, and my star ascending;
I was immature, foolish, yet full of life;
I thought that the future was never ending."

"My years have made me wiser than you" said the old man
"Though I know you do not wish to think it so;
If you listen carefully to me I can tell you things
That for your life ahead you really ought to know."

"Why should I listen to you" said the youth,
"What can you tell me that I do not already know,
Unlike you I am swift of foot and sharp of mind
And if I need to learn something I'll learn it as I go"

And so the youth set off and lived his life,
A journey full of many highs and many lows
Full of things he wished he had and hadn't done
And year by passing year he'd older grow.

"I was young once," said the father to the son,
"I too dreamed of love, luxury, and my star ascending;
I was immature, foolish, yet full of life;
I thought that the future was never ending."

E J Dawkins

16

WHY ?

I have sometimes stopped and wondered why
There are billions of stars up in the sky
And why we live and why we die;
Have YOU ever stopped and wondered why ?

And at night when I lay upon my bed
With thoughts of life running through my head,
I ask myself why do each of us, unthinking, race headlong
To a somewhere that those who came
before us have all gone.

After life there must be more, there must be more,
If not, then what on earth are we living for ?
Nobody asks to be born, yet nobody wants to die,
For each of us to exist there must be some reason why.

But is there a reason for life,
Or is life just a stupid game ?
Surely life cannot be pointless,
For it to be pointless would be totally insane.

And if there is God who holds us dear
Will he give us life eternal when we are gone from here ?
So when I die I hope that my "soul" will live on
To understand the reason why, why I lived and why I died.

E J Dawkins

17

WHY, WHY ?

Why are we here to live our lives,
To walk upon this world of ours ?
Is it to praise our Gods and seek an intangible salvation,
Or is it just to gaze in awe at the wonders of all creation ?

And when I look into a star filled sky
It makes me stop and contemplate the reason why,
Until my mind explodes with the countless possibilities,
Needing an answer for my soul to take into eternity.

We must be here for a reason, a purpose,
The near impossibility of our existence demands to know.
Dust to dust we surely are
And in between must we living ghosts "just come and go".

E J Dawkins

18

QUESTIONS IN LIFE

WHAT must be done ?
WHEN can they do it ?
WHY must it be done ?
WHERE can they do it ?
HOW will it be done ?
WHO the hell will do it !

ATOMS

The atoms that make up you and me
Will be around for all eternity;
And if atoms have a memory
There will be billions and billions
of you and me around for all eternity !

THE CAT

The cat sat on the mat,
The cat shat on the mat,
The cat sat and shat on the mat,
Oh shit !

COMMUTING TO LONDON IN 1976

I'm on the 06.30 train to St Pancras again
And the heavens are throwing rain down;
The carriage is old and I'm tired and cold
And it's a bloody long way into town !

E J Dawkins

FALLING OUT OF LOVE

Falling out of love is the saddest thing,
When it starts you barely know it's happening,
A virus called "Indifference" enters your heart
And slowly it begins to tear your world apart.

Memories start to fade of when you first met,
Of that exciting time the virus first makes you forget,
Of that yearning for being together
whenever you were apart
And when to hold each other with a kiss
did something crazy to your heart.

Gone now are the days when you were sure
that you would be together for life;
The days that you spent planning for the
future, as partners, husband, wife.
Gone now are the days when you always
smiled into each other's eyes,
When you laughed at each other, joked,
and never told each other lies.

The virus now mutates and multiplies.
Thinking about the act of passion dies.
Irritation and impatience with each other now sets in
And each other's funny little habits
now cease to raise a grin.

(Continued)

You begin to believe that you've loved the
wrong person for all those years
And the thought of loosing one another
no longer brings you to tears.
Then it happens, a betrayal or a bitter
quarrel, and cruel words are said;
And the virus now completely consumes
you and your love is dead.

But the heart will recover with the passing of time
For if a heart looses love then new love it must find;
Because a heart without love is no heart at all
And to be in love is the one overwhelming
emotion that surpasses all.

E J Dawkins

FRIENDSHIP

Whenever something has made you gloomy or sad,
Whenever someone has made you angry or mad,
Whenever you're happy and want to play,
Whenever you just want to break away,
Let me take your hand, I'm your friend.

Whenever you've won a hard fought game,
Whenever you've had a moment of fame,
Whenever a child is born to you,
Whenever in adversity you've won through,
Let me shake your hand, I'm your friend

Whenever you're anxious or in a stew,
Whenever you don't know what to do,
Whenever someone's been spiteful or mean to you,
Whenever you're lonely or need someone to talk to,
Give me your hand, I'm your friend.

Whenever you're sick or feeling tired and blue,
Whenever you need help in what you have to do,
Whenever you've had a dreadful day,
Whenever you just want the world to go away,
Put your hand in mine, I'm your friend.

Whenever you're depressed or in despair,
Whenever you just need someone to care,
Whenever a loved one is ill or fades away
Whenever you need support in any way,
I'll give you my hand, I'm your friend.

And when your life is near its end,
I'll hold your hand because I'm your friend.

E J Dawkins

22

LIVES

Some people have lived extraordinary lives
And their lives live on and on;
Their deeds, their writings, their spoken words
Are remembered long after they are gone.

But I am just an ordinary man,
I have led an ordinary life,
And no one will remember me,
Yet still I have lived a life.

E J Dawkins

WE BRITISH

For centuries upon our sceptred isles
Ancient, unknown, tribes lived and survived.
Then came waves of strangers from across the sea
Who mixed the blood and sowed the seed.

Mix brain of Roman and strength of Celt
With essence of Angles, Saxons, Vikings,
Norman French as well;
Add to this mixture a common mother tongue,
Thus the building of a nation had begun.

Then fling this mongrel nation out across the seas
To explore, our wealth and knowledge to increase;
Bring order to many a far off land,
Building an empire, vast and grand.

We British then a revolution began
With iron and steel and coal and steam;
With scientists and engineers we changed the world,
Building cities into which people streamed.

Then came a time of turmoil
And we fought in two long and bloody wars
Which left the world in such chaos
As had never been seen before.

Our empire and influence then waned
And we retreated back to our isles,
But the world now speaks our mother tongue
Which it will do for quite a while !

E J Dawkins

24

STRANGERS ON THE UNDERGROUND

(Written when I worked for London Underground)

Here we sit, face to face,
A couple of rats in the rat race,
Rattling through time and space
Below old London town.

We try not to look into each other's eyes,
Is she poor or happy, rich or wise ?
If she spoke would it be truth or lies ?
Our thoughts drift on and on.

Oh stranger, stranger, can you not see
That each morning when you sit in front of me,
You show no warmth, no friendliness, no humanity,
Anonymously must we part ?

Communication here cannot be found,
"No talking on the Underground",
By this silent law we're bound,
But we will meet again.

E J Dawkins

25

BECAUSE OF LOVE

So many hearts have been broken;
So many tears have been shed;
So many bitter words written;
So many untruths have been said;

YET

So many risks have been taken;
So many struggles have been won;
So many passionate words spoken;
So many moving songs have been sung;

BUT

So many feelings have been hidden;
So many emotions have been displayed;
So many precious lives given;
So many sacrifices have been made;

BECAUSE OF LOVE

E J Dawkins

26

MUSIC

We cannot see it but it creates images in our mind,
We cannot taste it yet it has many flavours,
We cannot touch it yet it touches us,
We cannot smell it but like a lovely scent it lingers.

Through our ears it enters our senses
It hypnotizes us, setting thoughts and memories in motion;
It permeates through every organ,
every muscle, every limb,
Bouncing between head and heart,
it speaks to our emotions.

It carries us away to times and places that
Our mind remembers from yesterday and long ago;
It always takes us back to happy times and places,
Never back to times and places where we do not want to go.

We hear it on the radio, on television
and from the cinema screen;
We hear it almost every day and sometimes,
at night, in a blissful dream;
We hear it sing and play the songs, melodies
and symphonies that each of us adore;
May music be everlasting, may it play for evermore.

E J Dawkins

27

THOUGHTS

Each day of our existence our senses see,
Their messages ceaselessly entering our brains,
Arriving and departing at the speed of light
As we journey swiftly through our meagre days.

But our thoughts are the creations of our minds
And we use them in diverse and different ways;
Yet we seldom stop to document our deepest thoughts,
Just let them slip, neglected, into time and space.

But we are unlike all other living things upon this earth,
Our minds let us remember, reason and communicate,
We can feel emotions that can shake us to our very core
And dream of and imagine things beyond our gaze.

Yet when our consciousness departs this world forever
And what we were returns to the
place from whence it came,
All that will remain of our deepest, innermost, thoughts
Will be those that we've implanted in our childrens' brains.

E J Dawkins

28

SUICIDAL

(Written, too late, for a friend who committed suicide)

It's a dark place that you have gone
to, a dark place of despair,
And nobody, it seems, can ever reach you there;
A place where nobody understands what's in your mind,
A place where your mind no longer any peace can find,
Where your inner being cannot raise
itself to face each passing day,
Where you look forward and see nothing
but obstacles in your way,
Where your mind cannot release itself
from an endless spiral of despair,
And the Black Dog of depression snarls
and barks to keep you there.

But for the sake of all those in your life who have
held you close and those who now hold you dear,
You must make your mind fight the demons of self-
destruction that have driven you to despair.
Come back and enjoy life's simple pleasures once more;
Live life in each precious minute, as
you have never done before.
Your loving family and caring friends will reach out to you
if you reach out to them,
And together they will solve with you your every
real and imaginary problem.

E J Dawkins

29

LAUGHTER

It happens quite uncontrollably
Whenever we hear or see an hilarious absurdity.
Inside, our brain flicks on a switch
And our body starts to twitch;
Then it comes from somewhere deep inside,
This show of mirth we cannot hide,
Erupting like a fountain in full flow,
Laughter, we can't stop it, we just have to let it go !

This happy, joyful, glorious sound
That from our smiling mouth escapes,
Is like no other noise we make,
So uncontrollable, our body shakes,
And as our laughter bursts into the air,
Our composure's lost, but we don't care,
And those hearing it from not far away,
Well, they just have to smile, it lifts their day;

And when our laughter is all spent
We feel at peace, in deep content.
The leaders of this world should know
That to follow laughter is the way to go !

E J Dawkins

30

MOVING ON

I don't know when we finally decided to move,
To leave this house and go;
The reasons why we're moving we've told our friends,
The neighbours, well, they don't need to know.

This house is full of memories,
But our time here has now come and gone;
These four walls have done their job,
Now's the right time for us to be moving on.

We leave behind things that we no longer want, or need,
And an unfinished job or two,
No more planning what to do here next,
We're leaving for the experiences of living somewhere new.

We're both nervous and excited as to what
The future in our new home may hold,
But when revamping and refurbishing our new place
We must remember to be bold.

The next chapter of our life is waiting there
In our new home with its unknowns and change of scenery.
We're looking forward to making new memories there
And making it the place where we want to be.

E J Dawkins

31

ELLEN FERISH

Who was Ellen Ferish ?
She came without a name,
Born to the world one yesterday
Through her mother's pain.

A child as other children,
She played and skipped and sang,
She dreamed her dreams and whispered wishes,
With innocence her laughter rang.

As our earth span round and round she grew
And her innocence was lost,
Her eyes ceased to glow with wonder,
By events her mind was tossed.

She had her children, knew her place,
Thought not of the reasons why,
Existence continuing day by day,
Anonymously to live; anonymously to die.

Yet her being cannot be erased
For we are all immortal in our childrens' eyes;
She made no mark upon this earth
But nor, my friend, can you or I.

She was one of us who saw the stars,
Who smiled at sun and cried at rain,
Who's intelligence kept her alive,
Who's emotions caused her pain.

Who was Ellen Ferish ?
She came without a name,
Born to the world one yesterday
Through her mother's pain.

E J Dawkins

32

GOING CRUISING

Slowly we begin to move; with a shudder we are underway;
The hour has come, the tide is high
and to us the sea is calling.
And as we wave a last farewell the great
ship glides out into the swell,
Urged on towards an immense horizon
by the sea birds squawking.

Our ship is set to sail to different lands
To see sites and cities that no ancient mariner ever saw,
But we do not set off into the unknown
We are sailing seas that many now have sailed before.

And our ship is wondrous to behold,
No longer made of wood with canvas sails
to be blown by fickle winds across the seas,
But a mighty maritime marvel, born of man's ingenuity;
A self-powered metal monster, yet
graceful and beautiful to see.

For we are mariners of our time
And sail across the oceans in the height of luxury;
We are cruising to leave our daily
woes and worries behind us
We journey for the joy of living and
to create some memories.

(Continued)

And our fellow passengers are a cosmopolitan crowd,
Likewise, from many lands come the
members of our obliging crew,
All brought together for a nautical
adventure all too brief in time,
But knowing there will be camaraderie and
merriment as we sail across the blue.

And as behind us the thin black line of
land disappears beneath the waves
We explore the ship and settle into the
cosy cabin where we'll sleep;
Then slowly, as the earth turns, we are
enveloped by the darkness on the night
And we sail on to dream amongst the
stars upon the surface of the deep.

E J Dawkins

34

AGAIN

There are places I have been to
And people I have known,
These I want to see again
But now my time has flown.

There are things I want to do again
And experiences to have again
And days I want to live again,
But now my time has flown.

There are thoughts I want to think again
And emotions I want to feel again
And to fall passionately in love again,
But now my time has flown.

Yet Time now whispers in my ear
"These things you want, you have;
These people, places, your every act still exist,
They remain alive forever in the past".

E J Dawkins

35

OLD MAN STORM

He begins with a gentle sneeze, sending
his raindrops falling from the night,
They bounce on the roads and pavements
and shatter on the bright streetlights,
Filling every nook and cranny,
Gurgling in the gutters with delight.

But soon we hear his booming cough of thunder,
Bright flashes of his anger are showing him the way,
That sick and grumpy Old Man Storm is coming,
His game, called "Staying Dry", he'll make us play.

Up pop umbrellas from those who were prepared,
Others scurry for cover looking quite absurd,
And all around the raindrops dance
To a tune that can't be heard.

Frightened children cry and hide beneath
the safety of their bed covers,
Late night revellers seek sanctuary in shop
doorways, hiding there with others.
The curious look and wait for the next
flash of his anger to appear,
Then count the seconds till he coughs again
to tell if his heart is far away or near.

(Continued)

Eventually we hear his coughing easing,
As does the strength of his terrible sneezing,
Then as suddenly as he came he's gone,
Yet in the distance he grumbles on.

And of the pandemonium he brought
with him all that remains
Is the sound of his last raindrops
gently dripping down a drain;
And of the torment that came with him
we can do nothing but complain
But sometime in the future we will
have to play his game again.

E J Dawkins

37

AT THE POINT OF DEATH

What happens at the point of death ?
That instant of my last expired breath;
The moment the final thought runs through my head;
From living in this world, then dead.

In these final seconds when I die,
What last image will enter my eyes;
And will I smiling go, to a place I do not know,
Or will I struggle not to say goodbye ?

E J Dawkins

MY FRIEND THE SEA

Over the last hill it waited for me,
That vast enigma we call "the sea".
My eyes relaxed in its welcoming embrace
As a gentle breeze caressed my face,
And I smiled to see my friend once more
On another timeless, peaceful, shore.

My spirits lifted at just being there
And of my troubled world I ceased to care,
And as the waves spent kisses left the shore
I remembered my childhood days once more,
With rusty bucket and spade in hand
Making crumbling castles in the sand.

Then other memories came back to me
Of happy times beside the sea;
Of noisy little seaside towns,
Where, in boarding houses, we stayed and bedded down;
Of seaside fun-fares filled with children's screams,
Full of the joy of life and of ice-cream.

Thoughts then came of my children's glee
Whenever we took them to see the sea,
Running up and down a sandy beach
Just keeping out of the water's reach,
Then shrieking when cold water
suddenly reached their feet
Tiptoeing then into the sea, each oncoming wave to greet.

Now, as an old man, I have come back once more
To see my friend again upon another windswept shore,
To hear it, smell it, feel it as many times before,
To gaze at it again in wonder and in awe,
To look to the horizon, where the sky meets the sea
And to dream of distant shores that I still yearn to see.

E J Dawkins

39

THE END OF DAYS

We have reached the end of days my friends;
The human race is nearly run;
And what difference to eternity have we made ?
The answer must be none !

In a flash of light we will have come and gone,
Our footprints will not remain;
But will we destroy ourselves
Before the natural ending of our game ?

E J Dawkins

THE FAT PUG

Staring into a half empty glass
of warm winter beer
I must have looked forlorn
and bereft of good cheer,
For the barmaid left the bar
and came and gave me a hug
"Cheer up" she said, "Its Christmas
and you're in The Fat Pug".

Somehow I had found my way
and stumbled into this little inn,
Leaving behind me a year of events
that for me had been quite grim;
What I needed was a drink
before the close of the day,
Hoping that it would help lift my mood,
make my "blues" go away.

"Here In The Fat Pug we only sell
happiness throughout the year,
I see your glass is nearly empty
let me get you one more beer.
There'll be live music in here
in a minute or two,
And if you ask them nicely
they'll sing a song just for you".

So I stayed and sang along to my favourite song
And we partied on until long after the closing time gong.
It was well after two when we were all told "No More !"
So the barmaid and I crept off to bed,
in her house, next door !

E J Dawkins

41

THERE'S SOMETHING THE MATTER WITH MY BRAIN

There's something the matter with my brain,
It's nearly driving me insane;
It never stops talking to me, it never
gives me a moment's peace,
The only time I can get away from it is
when I close my eyes and go to sleep.

Each morning when I awake feeling
relaxed, warm and cosy,
And with nothing in my head,
It tells me that I must get up, no time to waste,
But all I really want to do is stay in bed.

Each day it tells me what I must wear and eat,
And how to talk and act,
It instructs me in what and what not to do
And that's a blooming fact !

It sometimes gives me awful, dreadful thoughts
To test my morality,
It often makes me say the most stupid things,
With no apology.

And when I'm sure it gives me doubts,
It creates stress and anxiety,
And when I'm depressed it never helps,
Then only the outside world can rescue me.

(Continued)

It fights with my emotions
And tries to stop me being me,
The only thing, it seems, it's useful for
Is to store my memories.

Me and my brain will have to sort things out
Or else insanity,
So I'll go to bed and sleep on it,
Unless it wakes me up to pee !

E J Dawkins

43

LONELINESS

We enter our world from our mother's womb
And instantly strong helping hands are there;
We are nurtured by many along life's way
By loving families and friends who care.

We spend our hum-drum lives at work and play;
Active, attentive, animated every day.
Then suddenly someone special comes our way
And we share our lives with them each passing day.

Children are born, they grow, then go,
And life slows down as older we grow.
Then comes that sad and dreadful day
When our life's partner slips away.

Suddenly solitude and silence
Except for the voice inside our head,
"Am I doomed to end my days in loneliness
Until I too am dead ?"

E J Dawkins

44

OLIVIA

(My Granddaughter)

Olivia, oh Olivia,
I wish you could tell me why, oh why,
You look at me that way
With those deep blue eyes.

A wide-eyed bonny babe with no words yet to speak
To tell me, truly, what you think and see
When with those big blue eyes you stare
And look so quizzically at me.

Although you are only a baby, a cute little mite,
When you look at me that way is it in horror or delight ?
What thoughts are running through your head
What words would you say if they could be said ?

But when I look at you let me tell you what I see,
I see the child, the girl, the woman that you could be;
I see the wonder of life within those deep blue eyes,
I see a little bit of me in you and how, once, I used to be.

Although in years you are not yet one,
Let me tell you this of the present and of the years to come;
You are loved and those loving you will
guide you through your years,
And with that love no one can harm you, have no fears.

Those deep blue eyes will see so many things,
And who knows what the future brings,
Yet the future is there for you to see,
But, if you can, stop sometimes and remember me.

Love "Gandad"

E J Dawkins (March 2020)

45

WHERE DID WE COME FROM ?

Where did we come from ?
I think we thought we knew.
"We came from specks of stardust
when the universe was new".

We came from stardust touching stardust
When the Sun shone brightly on the sea
And minute creatures sprang into life
And multiplied in the oceans and the seas.

Mystery surrounds the next few billion years
When strange creatures left the seas
And giant lizards began to roam the Earth
But still no sign of you and me !

Then suddenly the giant lizards ceased to be
And many more millions of years passed bye
Before, as if from nowhere, mammals
appeared upon the Earth
But still, my friend, no sign of you or I.

Now we've been told that we have evolved, directly,
From a hairy mammal we humans call "an Ape",
But if this is true how can it be that the likes of you and me
Have brains and bodies that can do
astounding things like no other Ape !

Were we created by a God or are we
the spawn of ancient aliens
from outer space ?
For there are things about what we are and where
we came from that I just don't understand;
We've solved the riddle of the planets and stars and how
the universe began,
So why the mystery of how we came to be and who or what
created man ?

E J Dawkins

46

AND THEY TELL ME THERE'S A GOD

Little children suffer every day in
ways only little children can,
Bullied, brutalized, beaten, butchered,
by bystanders betrayed;
People are born disabled, are killed by
cancers, die with dementia.
And they tell me there's a loving God.

Wars follow wars, killing communities,
families and friends.
Animosity and hatred bring genocide,
murder and bloodshed.
Torture, cruelty and thuggery go unpunished and ignored.
And they tell me there's a God of peace.

Diseases, plagues and poisons spread
pain and death in many lands.
Volcanoes, earthquakes, storms,
tsunamis bring destruction,
The wrath of mother nature plays many
a cruel and spiteful hand.
And they tell me there's a merciful God.

Thoughtlessness, selfishness, spitefulness lead to
senseless, needless harm;
Theft, fraud and corruption also do their best.
Mankind is left to maim itself in so many different ways.
And they tell me there's a wise God.

(Continued)

They tell me that there's only one almighty God,
Who made our world, the universe
and everything that's in it.
He gave us life to live freely in this world,
He made us all, and what is more, they
tell me, He made us in his image.

But why create us, and this world,
The troubles of which He surely knows?
They tell me that He cares for us
But his care for us He seldom shows.

So if I meet this almighty God on my dying day
With him I'll take issue and have many words to say.

E J Dawkins

48

JOYOUS EMOTIONS

Words spoken in a baby's eyes;
Music that makes you cry;
Good deeds done by strangers;
Memories that never die;
Retribution for an evil act;
The exposing of a lie;
Embracing the one you love;
Returning from a sad goodbye;
Each spark joyous emotions
To ease a troubled mind.

E J Dawkins

LUST FULFILLED

Quickly we shed our clothes
And as we were born we come together;
Hands feeling for intimate places,
Hands feeling as our instincts dictate.
Breathing quickens as we kiss and kiss
Hearts pounding we eagerly entwine
Delirious in our passionate embrace.

Man now enters woman again and again;
Senses explode at the climax of our passion,
Our bodies shake with ecstatic spasms.
Then we collapse exhausted and roll apart,
Look at each other with a knowing smile
And just let our thoughts drift into space.

E J Dawkins

50

LIFE'S TOO SHORT

"Life's too short" has so often, in jest, been said,
Yet we never really knew that these words were oh so true,
Unaware that our years were slipping swiftly bye,
Vanishing in the blink of eternity's eye.

And too often we ignored the little joys and curious things
That each passing day did so often bring;
Too busy striving, surviving, day by day,
Not noticing the weeks that we just flittered away.

Then in old age we realize, too late,
That we had wasted too many of our days,
Constantly looking forward to tomorrow
Not always relishing what we had today.

But there is one thing that brings us solace
And seems to lengthen our last days,
And that is to spend time with our grandchildren,
To watch them grow, to share their days.

E J Dawkins

51

FEELING THE SEASONS

(In my boyhood, in England, in the 1950s and 1960s)

If only I had the words to describe the
feeling of a perfect day in spring;
When soft clouds blown by a fresh wind
bring an unexpected squally shower
That anoints with life each sprouting
plant and wildly budding flower.
Then, in an instant, the sun creates a rainbow
in summer colours yet to come
And lifts into the air the perfume of spring
that my senses truely welcome;
And as my mind comes alive with expectations
of what the year ahead may bring
I'm glad that I've lived to see, once more,
another perfect day in spring.

If only I had the words to describe the
feeling of a perfect summer's day;
When the sun on high has driven all
the rain clouds far away
And its warmth from sunrise to sunset
is felt throughout the day,
And all around the flowers bloom in a symphony of scents
And the shades of green of each plant
and tree are truly heaven sent,
And as the summer sun warms and relaxes
me, as I in a peaceful garden lay,
I'm glad that I have lived to see, once more,
another perfect summer's day.

(Continued)

If only I had the words to describe the
feeling of a perfect autumn day;
When leaves fall unwanted from the
trees in countless shades
of brown and red and yellow
And the once bright summer sun in autumn's
damp and misty air has mellowed,
And from country hedgerows and woodlands
the last fruits of summer are
quickly gathered in,
And overhead summer birds fly south
for warmth leaving cold
winter to the plucky little robin;
And as, in the evening twilight, I light a bonfire of dead
leaves and withered summer flowers thrown away,
I'm glad that I've lived to see, once more,
another perfect autumn day.

If only I had the words to describe the
feeling of a perfect winter's day;
When the air is freezing cold and the
cloudless sky is crystal clear
And the overnight snow has covered my
world in a sparkling white veneer,
And each passing stranger smiles at me as
their warm breath turns to steam
And the snow muffles the noises of the day
and makes my dirty world seem clean,
And as virgin snow crunches beneath my feet
as homeward, at dusk, I make my way,
I'm glad that I've lived to see, once more,
another perfect winter's day.

E J Dawkins

CLOUDS

As the sun climbs over the horizon they are there
Floating silently in the morning air.
They set the scene for each new day
And with our daily moods they always play.

Unnoticed they subtly change with each passing minute;
Unexpectedly they change with every passing hour;
A mystical, magical presence floating in the sky;
They hold us at their mercy with their atmospheric power.

Sometimes throwing down torrential rain
That can last for many hours;
Sometimes just soft and gently rain
From a passing, breezy, shower.

Sometimes they cover the sky
In a misty cloak of murky grey;
Sometimes in a black and foreboding cloak
That foretells a storm is on its way.

Sometimes they are just white smudges or wispy streaks
High up on the surface of a blue, blue sky;
Sometimes they are like gigantic puffs of steam
From some ethereal steam train that has just chuffed bye.

Yet when the sun shines on them on a summer's day,
To give them many merging shades of grey and white,
Our imagination sees within their billowing shapes
Faces, strange creatures, sleeping giants,
which surprise and fill us with delight.

(Continued)

And at sunset their colours change from white and grey
To vibrant melting shades of pink and grey
and red and orange, of indigo and yellow;
Which please our eyes and calm our hearts
And we feel relaxed, content and mellow.

And as with the loss of the light of the sun
They fade from view and disappear,
We sleep and dream with them in the darkness of the night
Until, with the dawn's new light, once more they re-appear.

E J Dawkins

55

A POEM

If only I could write a poem
To give me total peace of mind;
A poem that would do the same
For the rest of human kind.

A poem that would eradicate
The stress and worries of each day;
A poem that, when recalled, would make each person smile
And send them content and cheerful on their way.

A poem to tell the world
How good it is to be alive;
A poem to destroy despondency,
Each person's inner spirit to revive.

For poetry can touch the heart
And speak words of wisdom to the mind;
It can stir buried thoughts and emotions
And bring back memories of happy times.

But alas I've tried and failed to write a poem
To dispel the anxieties of each new day,
Yet each of us know a poem, a rhyme, a verse
That can lift our spirits, make us smile
and brighten up our day.

E J Dawkins

56

THIRTY THOUSAND SUNSETS

There were thirty thousand sunsets in my life,
Planet "Earth" span round for me so many times,
Each sunset brought to an end another day,
Each day that would be forever mine.

Each day never seen before and never seen again,
Each segment, fraction, moment of each day to live,
And visions of special days I stored away, in
memories and dreams,
To comfort and console me in the after life
where next I'll live.

My life is held for eternity in time, in past rotations
of my world
In its celestial orbit around a small bright star
we humans call the Sun.
I saw thirty thousand sunsets
Then my life on Earth was done.

E J Dawkins